Humanity's Desire for Freedom

Poetic Thoughts

by O.K. Fatai

Published by OK Publishing

Wellington, New Zealand

Email: OK.Publishingnz@gmail.com

Full catalogue in print data may be obtained from the National Library of New Zealand

ISBN-13: 978-0-473-51139-5

Dedication

To all those who had shown that we have an inner journey of freedom matters in life.

CONTENTS

Acknowledgements

I appreciate the help of my family and friends who value the importance of living as a people who uphold freedom in their journey.

it's a journey

freedom is about going
on a journey

a journey of discovery

discovery of what it means
to be you

discovery of your destiny

discovery of your ancestors
discovery of your goals

discovery of your ambitions
discovery of your talents

discovery of your inner desires
it is a journey towards freedom

for lives that have the
freedom to journey

journey towards self discovery,
are lives

that have freedom in their cores.

internal dialogue

we all have strange feelings sometime
feelings of alienation

feelings of disempowerment
feelings of discouragement

feelings of despair
feelings of joy

feelings of euphoria
feelings of loneliness

when we have those
strange feelings

we need to be free
to dialogue

with those feelings

and explore those feelings
for when we are engaging

in observations

and dialogue with
our inner strange feelings

we are in a state of freedom

confidence

be confident
for when the day is gone

and the sky looks bleak
the confident will strive on

and hope for another day
that will strike a chord

that resonate freedom

be confident
for when the wind blows

and the mountain shakes
with violent blows

that steaks the show
be confident

for the wind will be mild
and the mountains will be stable

for in confidence
you will find freedom

the confidence to
speak your mind

the confidence to
pursue your dreams

the confidence to

fight on

the confidence to
fill your spirit

in confidence
you will find freedom

shared

freedom is a
value to be shared

freedom is a
virtue to be given

freedom is a
diamond to be shined

shined not in the
face of nothing

but in the face of
opposition

and denial

shined not in the
army of the light

but in darkness and a
land filled
with chaos

never dim

freedom is light
that shall never dim

for in itself it is
divine in essence

for the divine works
to free people up

so when you fight
for freedom

be assured that the
divine works with you

for freedom is a divine
quality

that never dims in itself
even in the land of

oppression and violence

freedom will one day
rule

for freedom is powerful
and never dims in its light

never waver in its shine.

more than knowledge

freedom is more
than the mere

knowledge that
we all deserve

to have some
degree of freedom

for freedom is a
right that everyone

should experience

but reality is
freedom can sometimes

become a scarce commodity

as if it is something
that is allowed only in portion

but freedom when it is
fully experienced

really shows that
we are fully human.

fall short

it is human to
fall
short of
what is expected of us

it happens all the time

at work and at home

with friends and with family

but the beauty of
falling short is that

we are allowed to fall
short of expectations

and we are encouraged
to keep on trying

the knowledge that
we are allowed to fall short

and the belief that
we can keep on trying

is evidence of the
beauty of having

freedom.

a gift

freedom is a gift
for all humanity

we have that gift
right from the beginning

when that gift is
abused
it is also an act of
challenge to the giver

of humanity's freedom

we are here to live
the life of freedom

we were given as rights

we are here to
make use of the freedom

that was gifted to us
so why choose to
build walls of violence
to stop us from
using the freedom

that doesn't really
belong to you

for the giver of
freedom will guide

us in how we should
use that freedom responsibly.

just

freedom is the
passport that enables
us to engage

in what is just and good

freedom is the
gift that enables
us to live

within the law of the land

and freedom is a
gift that promotes justice
and peace,

it promotes responsibility
and love

for freedom that is
abused is not really the freedom

that is expected of us.

challenges

there are lots of challenges
that we face in life

but the ability to face those
challenges and be able to

do something about it
in ways that inspire others

speaks volumes about having
the freedom to face adversity

and having the freedom to face
the darkness in life and see daylight

in its fullness.

enables

freedom is an enabler
of people to reach their destiny

for when we have freedom
we are free to pursue our dreams

with eagerness and determination
but so many countries

have chosen that the freedom to
pursue dreams is not important

as they do not believe in true freedom
but beware of the march of time

and the progress that humanity have
for one day everyone will have the freedom

to pursue their dreams in life.

when we face

sometimes we face challenges
and when we face those

challenges head on
without fear of others

we experience an aspect

of freedom

that aspect of freedom
is called courage

sometimes we face challenges
and we decide to

overcome those challenges
with bold action, owning
what we do

without fear of others

then we are experiencing
as aspect of freedom

that aspect of freedom is
called determination

for when we have the
courage to pursue

and the determination to push on
we are beginning to see the many shining

facets of freedom.

sometime we have burdens

we all encounter some kind of
burdens in our journey

whether it is because of some
pains we had experienced

or because we face personality
challenges from others

or because of wrongs we encounter
from someone else

and the burdens all come in all
types of forms and shapes

and when we encounter those
burdens we have the desire

to fight them until we win the war
or totally overcome the enemy

sometimes the best thing
we can do is to release the burden

for the act of releasing the
burden is an act of

someone who is free.

free to pursue

freedom is a journey of discovery
discovering one's talents and skills

discovering one's weaknesses and shortfalls
discovering one's destiny and future

discovering one's family and relatives
discovering the world and community

discovering the environment and nature
discovering truths and facts of life

discovering religions and spirituality
and when we have success in

discovering who we are

then the soul is free to
have adventures and journey

to achieve and pursue
what we have discovered.

a gift

freedom is a precious gift
it is meant to be used without being abused

it is meant to be guided and guarded
it is a gift for all the children of nature

it is a gift that can easily be abused
and that's why there is guidance

as to how we enjoy this precious gift
we are stewards to this gift

we are to enjoy this gift
for it is a shining and gift that can

be easily taken away.

used with care

freedom if not used carefully
have the ability to wreck havoc
a person's life

for freedom, in order to flourish in society
needs to be used with care
it is a gift to enjoy

the various diamonds of freedom
it is never a license to oppress
it is never a license to take lives

it is never a license to destroy
it is never a license to suppress
it is never a license to silence

for when freedom is used without care
society will end up in chaos and violence.

can take us

freedom can take us to the moon and back
for freedom is like a rocket

that enables us to explore and journey
because we have freedom of thoughts

freedom can take us to the heart of the soul
for freedom is like a prayer

that enables us to know what lies in the soul
freedom can take us to the stars

for freedom is like a shining light
that can travel many miles in a second

freedom is really the precious gift
that humanity must all treasure.

a huge gift

when we receive an important gift
it is great to receive that gift with a heart

of gratitude and thanks
freedom is a gift of great value

that words of gratitude or thanks
may never be enough to express appreciation

let me suggest a good way to express appreciation
for the gift of freedom that we enjoy

it is to use the gift of freedom with the appreciation
of taking responsibility in how

we use this huge and important gift.

it is not

freedom is not like a prison
that enables those inside to be free

freedom is not like a jail
that gives security to those inside

freedom is not a gaol or a confinement
rather freedom is the ability to fly

and enjoy the beauty of the universe
freedom is the ability to make mistakes

and be free to be yourself
not within the confinement of a prison or jail

but within the vastness of the universe.

it is part

freedom is part of the family of humanity
it was there from the beginning of time

we were free to make mistakes
we were free to take responsibility

we were free to be who we are
we were free to explore and journey the world

we were free to express our thoughts
we were free to settle and build our lives

it is a right that should have never been taken away

for many of us.

it is there

freedom is there for us to enjoy
freedom is there for us to take care of

freedom is there for us to be steward of
freedom is there for us to protect

freedom is there for us to appreciate
freedom is there for us to adore

freedom is there for us to explore
freedom is there for us to relish

freedom is there for us to possess
freedom is there for us to experience

for freedom is right that was planted
within the deepness of the soul

and the soul longs for it
and the soul will fight for it.

if we desire

if we desire our own freedom
we must also desire for others
freedom as well

for inequity is the product
of exercising your own freedom

and never seeing it in the lives of someone else
and when there is inequity of freedom

society will decent into one of chaos
disorder and turmoil

for freedom is an honour
not only to achieve but more than that

to gift away to others less fortunate in society
for freedom is never an olympic torch to possess

for just one person but an olympic torch to pass on
for the benefit of everyone.

the air

freedom is like the air that we breathe
it is vast and is there for humanity

it is vital to the survival of the spirit
freedom is like the air that we breathe

it is an unseen but real force
it is there all the time

it is a gift for all of humanity.

we take liberty

we take liberty to be a responsible person
we take liberty to express our thoughts

we take liberty to make mistakes
we take liberty to be pursue our dreams

we take liberty to forgive
we take liberty to be courageous

we take liberty to pursue justice
we take liberty to give mercy

we take liberty to explore
we take liberty to be gracious

it comes because we have freedom.

to do

freedom gives us the opportunity
not to do anything that we would like to do

but to acknowledge the freedom we have
to take responsibility and love others

even if the others exercise their right
of freedom by expressing thoughts

that you don't agree with
for there are many who consider

you as a friend only if you agree
with them, but the responsibility

that lies with freedom gives you
the opportunity to respect others

and treat them well even if their
opinions are against you.

Other books by O.K. Fatai

1. Poems on Values to Succeed Worldwide in Life: Being Responsible
2. Poems on Values to Succeed Worldwide in Life: Courage
3. Poems on Values to Succeed Worldwide in Life: Good Families
4. Poems on Values to Succeed Worldwide in Life: Forgiveness
5. Poems on Values to Succeed Worldwide in Life: Good Friends
6. Poems on Values to Succeed Worldwide in Life: Grace
7. Poems on Values to Succeed Worldwide in Life: Hope
8. Poems on Values to Succeed Worldwide in Life: Humility
9. Poems on Values to Succeed Worldwide in Life: Joy
10. Poems on Values to Succeed Worldwide in Life: Justice
11. Poems on Values to Succeed Worldwide in Life: Life
12. Poems on Values to Succeed Worldwide in Life: Love
13. Poems on Values to Succeed Worldwide in Life: Mercy
14. Poems on Values to Succeed Worldwide in Life: Peace
15. Poems on Values to Succeed Worldwide in Life: Perseverance
16. Poems on Values to Succeed Worldwide in Life: Faith
17. Poems on Values to Succeed Worldwide in Life: Harmony with Nature
18. Poems on Values to Succeed Worldwide in Life: Education

More books by O.K. Fatai

1. Poems on Values to Succeed Worldwide in Life: Understanding and Wisdom
2. Poems on Values to Succeed Worldwide in Life: Work and Optimism
3. Poems on Values to Succeed Worldwide in Life: Adversity and Confidence
4. Poems on Values to Succeed Worldwide in Life: Listening and Diversity and Unity
5. Poems on Values to Succeed Worldwide in Life: Sharing and Honesty
6. Poems on Values to Succeed Worldwide in Life: Simplicity and Harmony
7. Poems on Values to Succeed Worldwide in Life: Unity in Diversity and Connections
8. Poems on Values to Succeed Worldwide in Life: Contentment and Acceptance
9. Poems on Values to Succeed Worldwide in Life: Excellence and Compassion
10. Poems on Values to Succeed Worldwide in Life: Generosity and Being Passionate
11. Poems on Values to Succeed Worldwide in Life: Gentleness and Trustworthy
12. Poems on Values to Succeed Worldwide in Life: Patience and Being Tactful
13. Poems on Values to Succeed Worldwide in Life: Purity and Integrity
14. Poems on Values to Succeed Worldwide in Life: Being Modest and Persistence
15. Poems on Values to Succeed Worldwide in Life: Respect and Loyalty

About the Author

O.K. Fatai is a poet and author from Wellington, New Zealand. He likes to spend time writing poems, especially ones that explore the different aspects of values and virtues that are widely accepted in different cultures today.

O.K. Fatai enjoys writing songs and some of his forthcoming books are song lyrics that look at different values and virtues and some of their appeal to us today. In his spare time, he writes short stories and novels. He is looking forward to sharing these stories with readers around the world, and he has already published some short stories and has more than ten forthcoming publications in children's literature. O.K. Fatai is writing novels for young adults and adults. He is also a playwright and has written and/or directed more than eight short plays.

He likes painting abstract art and enjoys the different interpretations of abstract paintings, especially when they reflect values and virtues. He is a photographer who likes to take photographs of nature and the environment, which has a special place in his heart. He is keen on filming and editing videos, plays musical instruments and is part of a local band.

O.K. Fatai is a volunteer at the United Nations and regional prisons in Wellington and, for many years has volunteered to more than ten other organizations. He works in the health sector and is a consultant for three different online companies, and the President and CEO of more than three businesses. He is also available as an external consultant to the United Nations, the European Bank for Reconstruction and Development, and the Asian Development Bank.